Jewish songs
for CGDA Mandola
or Tenor Banjo

Ondřej Šárek

Contents

Copyright © 2018 Ondřej Šárek
All rights reserved.
ISBN-13: 978-1719584074
ISBN-10: 1719584079

Introduction

This book features 20 songs.

The CGDA Mandola or Tenor Banjo managed to spread worldwide as well as Jewish music before. Moreover, Jewish music achieved to absorb different folk music, mostly European. For the reason you can meet here with beautiful
melodies in minor, which are not scales preferred by CGDA Mandola or Tenor Banjo playing.

Much joy in the disovery of Jewish songs.

How to read tablature

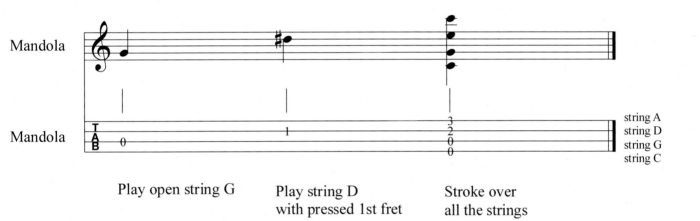

Play open string G

Play string D
with pressed 1st fret

Stroke over
all the strings

Adon Olam

arr: Ondřej Šárek

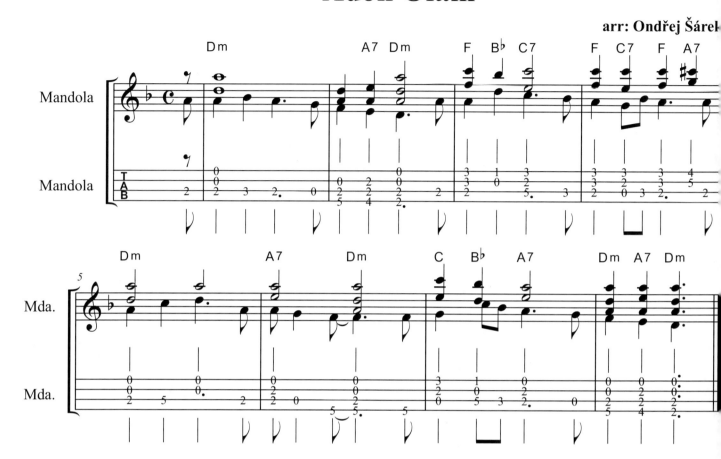

Adon Olam

arr: Ondřej Šárek

Amcha Jisrael

arr: Ondřej Šárek

Amcha Jisrael

arr: Ondřej Šárek

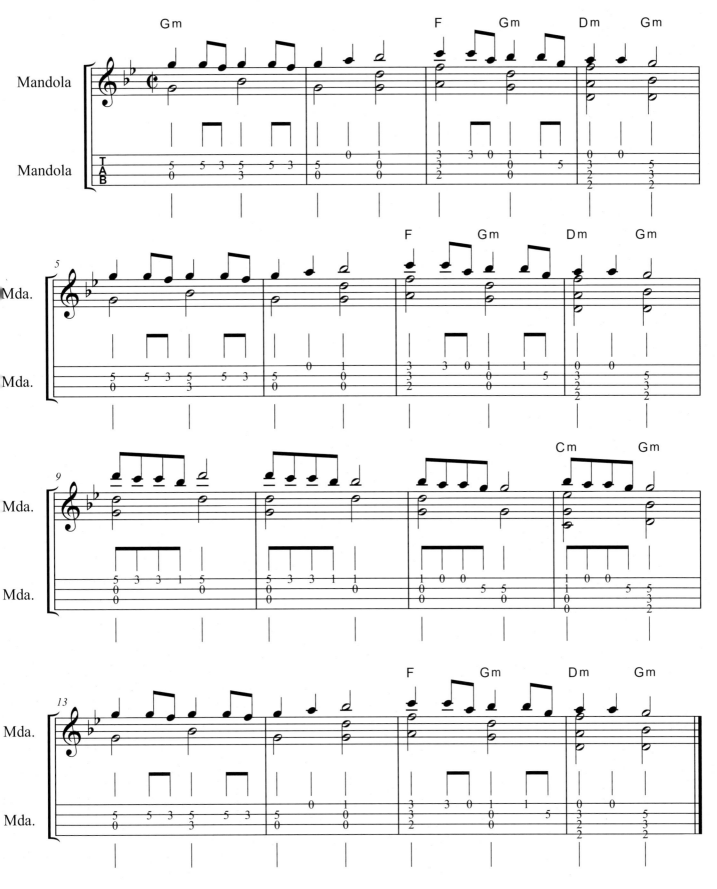

Artsa Alinu

arr: Ondřej Šárek

Artsa Alinu

arr: Ondřej Šárek

Avinu Malkenu

arr: Ondřej Šárek

Avinu Malkenu

arr: Ondřej Šárek

Chiribim Chiribom

arr: Ondřej Šárek

Chiribim Chiribom

arr: Ondřej Šárek

Copyright © 2018 Ondřej Šárek

Dajejnu

arr: Ondřej Šárek

Dajejnu

arr: Ondřej Šárek

David Melech Yisrael

arr: Ondřej Šárek

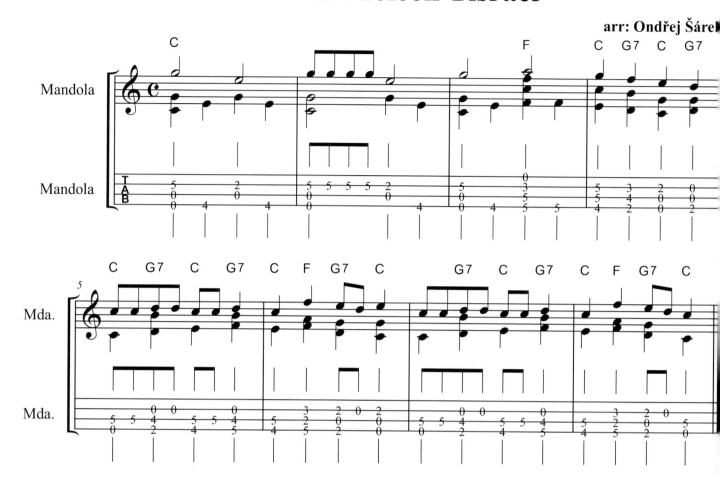

David Melech Yisrael

arr: Ondřej Šárek

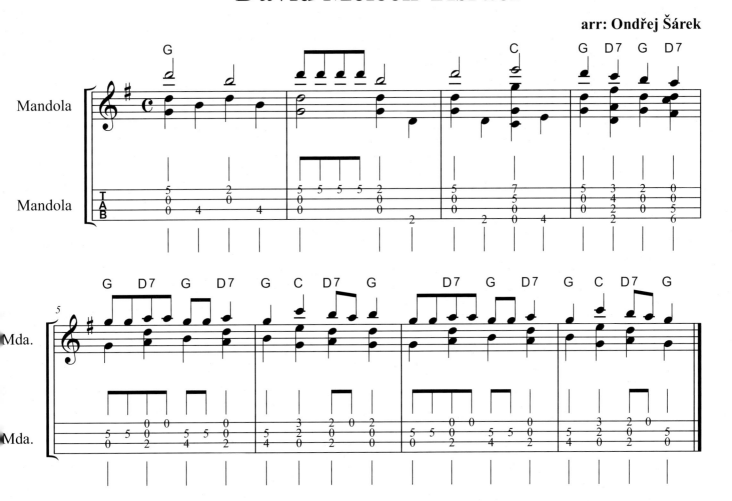

Hanukkah, Hanukkah

arr: Ondřej Šárek

Hanukkah, Hanukkah

arr: Ondřej Šárek

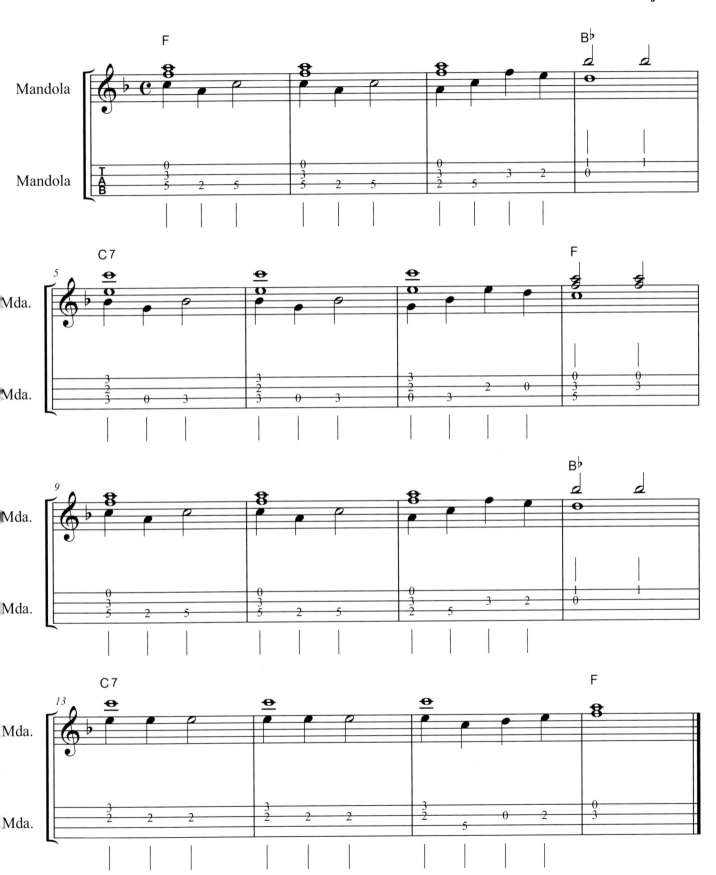

Hava Nagila

arr: Ondřej Šárek

Copyright © 2018 Ondřej Šárek

Hava Nagila

Hava Nagila

arr: Ondřej Šárek

Hava Nagila

Hevenu Shalom Aleichem

arr: Ondřej Šárek

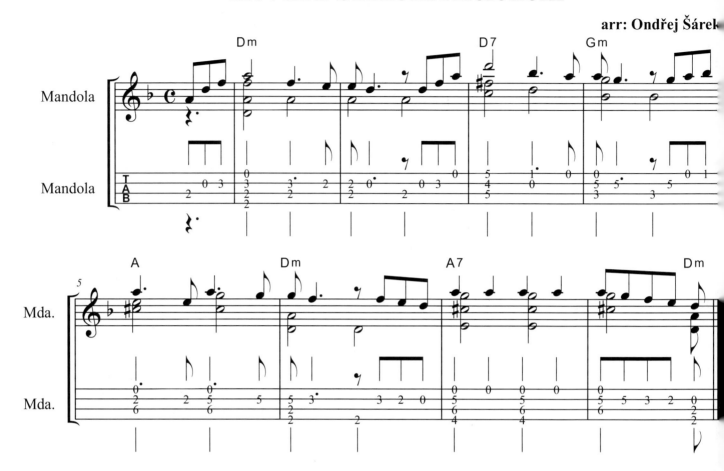

Hevenu Shalom Aleichem

arr: Ondřej Šárek

Hine Ma Tov

arr: Ondřej Šárek

Copyright © 2018 Ondřej Šárek

Hine Ma Tov

arr: Ondřej Šárek

Copyright © 2018 Ondřej Šárek

Chag Purim

arr: Ondřej Šárek

Chag Purim

arr: Ondřej Šárek

Kadesh Urchac

arr: Ondřej Šárek

Copyright © 2018 Ondřej Šárek

Kadesh Urchac

arr: Ondřej Šárek

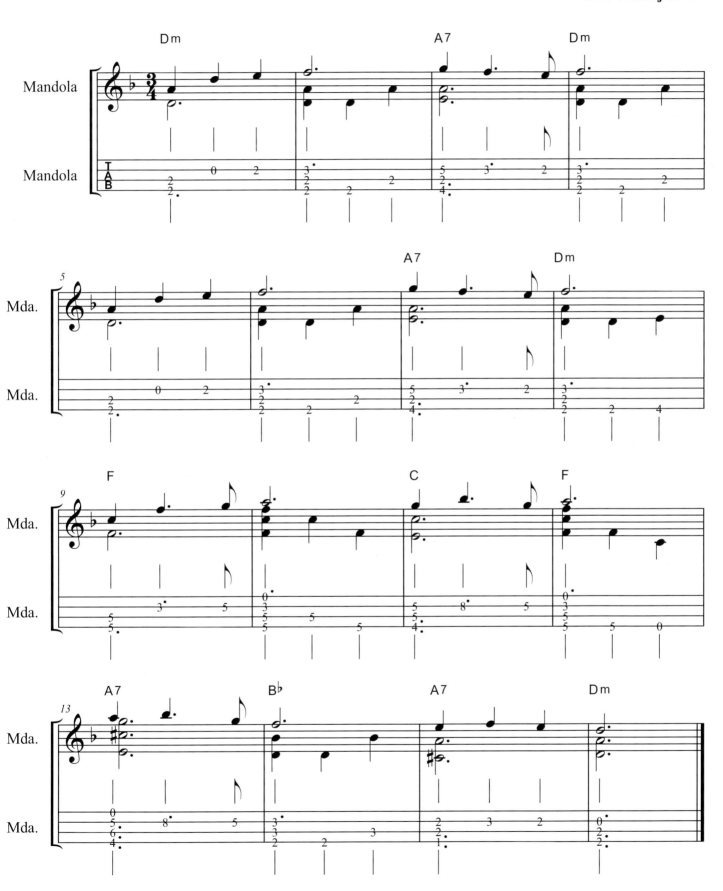

Copyright © 2018 Ondřej Šárek

Ner Li

arr: Ondřej Šárek

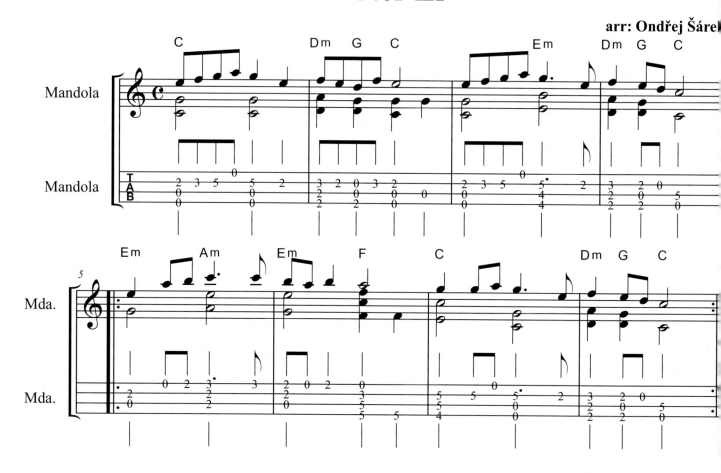

Ner Li

arr: Ondřej Šárek

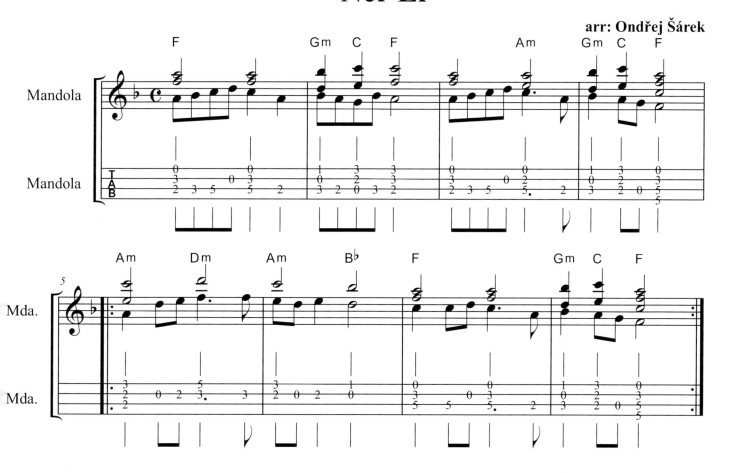

Nerot Shabat

arr: Ondřej Šárek

Copyright © 2018 Ondřej Šárek

Nerot Shabat

arr: Ondřej Šáre

Copyright © 2018 Ondřej Šárek

Nerot Shabat

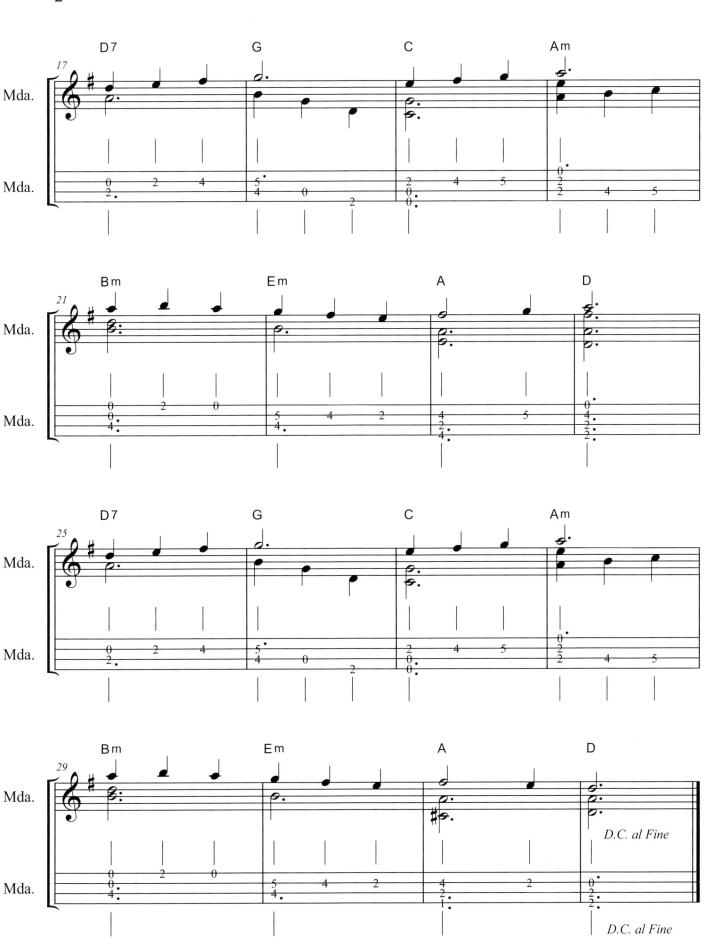

Shalom Chaverim

arr: Ondřej Šárek

Shalom Chaverim

arr: Ondřej Šárek

Copyright © 2018 Ondřej Šárek

Sevivon

arr: Ondřej Šárek

Sevivon

arr: Ondřej Šárek

Shema Israel

arr: Ondřej Šáre

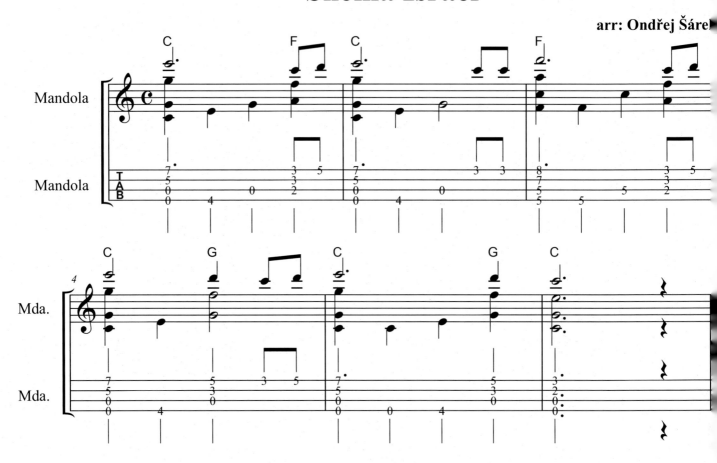

Shema Israel

arr: Ondřej Šárek

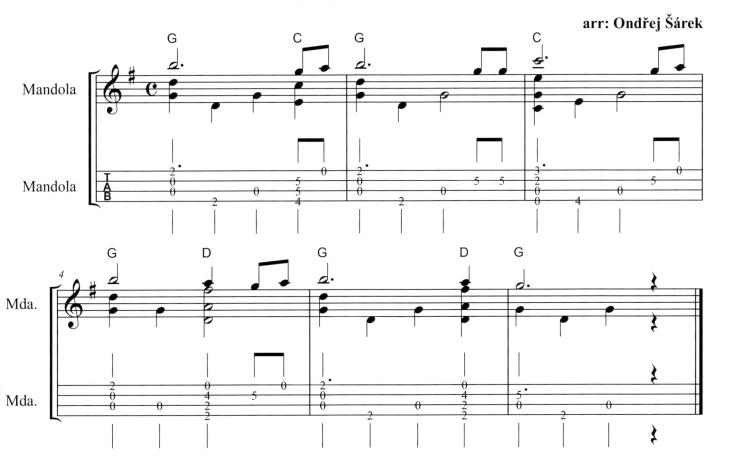

Tum Balalaika

arr: Ondřej Šárek

Tum Balalaika

arr: Ondřej Šárek

Yoshke Fort Avek

arr: Ondřej Šárek

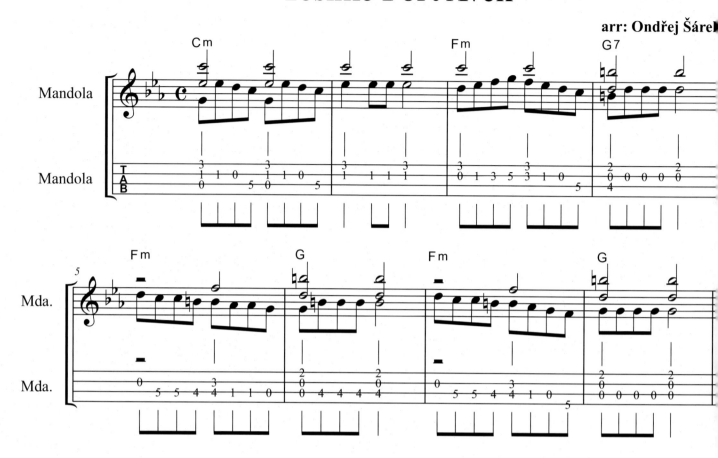

Yoshke Fort Avek

arr: Ondřej Šárek

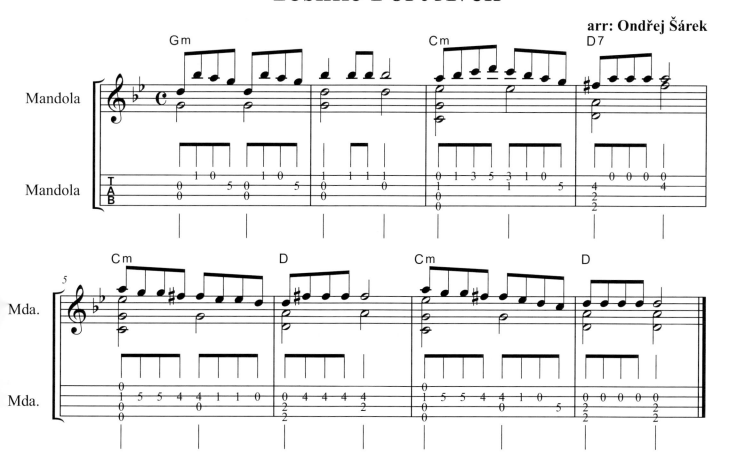

DADGAD Guitar
Czech Medieval DADGAD Guitar
The canons for DADGAD Guitar
Fingerpicking DADGAD Guitar Solo
The Czech Lute for DADGAD Guitar
Gregorian chant for DADGAD Guitar
Gregorian chant for flatpicking DADGAD Guitar
Gospel DADGAD Guitar Solos
Notebook for Anna Magdalena Bach and DADGAD Guitar
Czech Renaissance folk songs for DADGAD Guitar
Robert Burns songs for DADGAD Guitar

EADEAE Guitar
Fingerpicking EADEAE Guitar Solo

CGDGCD (Orkney tuning) Guitar
Gospel CGDGCD Guitar Solos
Notebook for Anna Magdalena Bach and CGDGCD Guitar
Gregorian chant for flatpicking CGDGCD Guitar
Fingerpicking CGDGCD Guitar Solo

EADGBE Guitar
Czech Medieval EADGBE Guitar
Gregorian chant for flatpicking EADGBE Guitar
The canons for EADGBE Guitar
The Czech Lute for EADGBE Guitar
Czech Renaissance folk songs for EADGBE Guitar
Robert Burns songs for EADGBE Guitar
18 Dance Tunes from Caslav Region for EADGBE Guitar
Czech Hymnbook for EADGBE Guitar
18 popular Czech Minuet for EADGBE Guitar

DADGBD (Double drop D tuning) Guitar
Gospel Double drop D tuning Guitar Solos
Notebook for Anna Magdalena Bach and Double drop D tuning Guitar

DADGBE (Drop D tuning) Guitar
Gospel Drop D tuning Guitar Solos
Notebook for Anna Magdalena Bach and Drop D tuning Guitar
Fingerpicking Drop D tuning Guitar Solo
Gregorian chant for flatpicking Drop D tuning Guitar
Robert Burns songs for Drop D tuning Guitar

Cut Capo (Partial Capo) Guitar
Cut capo flatpicking guitar songbook Gospel and Hymns I.
Cut capo flatpicking guitar songbook Gospel and Hymns II.
Cut capo flatpicking guitar songbook Christmas Carols
Cut capo flatpicking guitar songbook Jewish songs
Cut capo flatpicking guitar songbook Gregorian chant
Cut capo flatpicking guitar songbook Children's Songs

Mandolin
Czech Medieval Mandolin
Gregorian chant for flatpicking Mandolin
Czech Renaissance folk songs for Mandolin
Classical music for Mandolin

Christmas Carols for Crosspicking Mandolin
Robert Burns songs for Mandolin
Compositions for Mandolin
18 Dance Tunes from Caslav Region for Mandolin
Fingerpicking Mandolin or GDAE Ukulele Solo
Notebook for Anna Magdalena Bach and Fingerpicking Mandolin or GDAE Ukulele
10 songs from the years 1899-1920 for Mandolin
Czech Hymnbook for Mandolin
Boogie woogie patterns for Mandolin
Gospel for Mandolin
Jewish songs for Mandolin

Mandola or Tenor Banjo or Tenor Guitar (CGDA)
Classical music for Mandola or Tenor Banjo
18 Dance Tunes from Caslav Region for Mandola or Tenor Banjo
Robert Burns songs for Mandola or Tenor Banjo
Gregorian chant for Mandola or Tenor Banjo
Fingerpicking Mandola or Tenor Banjo
10 songs from the years 1899-1920 for CGDA Mandola
Czech Hymnbook for CGDA Mandola
Boogie woogie patterns for CGDA Mandola
Christmas Carols for Crosspicking Mandola or Tenor Banjo
Compositions for CGDA Mandola
Romantic Pieces by František Max Kníže for fingerpicking CGDA Tenor Guitar
Classical music for fingerpicking CGDA Tenor Guitar
Cut capo 2220 for CGDA tenor banjo, tenor guitar or mandola
Gospel for CGDA Mandola or Tenor Banjo
Jewish songs for CGDA Mandola or Tenor Banjo

Irish (GDAD) Bouzouki
Christmas Carols for Crosspicking GDAD Bouzouki
Classical music for GDAD Bouzouki
Czech Renaissance folk songs for GDAD Bouzouki
Josef Pekárek *Two Hanakian operas* for GDAD Bouzouki
Robert Burns songs for GDAD Bouzouki
18 Dance Tunes from Caslav Region for GDAD Bouzouki
Gregorian chant for GDAD Bouzouki
Compositions for GDAD Bouzouki
Gospel GDAD Bouzouki Solos
10 songs from the years 1899-1920 for GDAD Bouzouki
Czech Hymnbook for GDAD Bouzouki
Boogie woogie patterns for GDAD Bouzouki
Jewish songs for GDAD Bouzouki

Duet for Mandolin and other instrument
Notebook for Anna Magdalena Bach for Mandolin and instrument from the mandolin family
Notebook for Anna Magdalena Bach for Mandolin and EADGBE Guitar
Notebook for Wolfgang for Mandolin and instrument from the mandolin family
Notebook for Wolfgang for Mandolin and EADGBE Guitar

New Ukulele books

For C tuning ukulele
Classics for Ukulele (MB)
Ukulele Bluegrass Solos (MB)
Antonin Dvorak: Biblical Songs
Irish tunes for all ukulele
Gospel Ukulele Solos
Gregorian chant for Ukulele
The Czech Lute for Ukulele
Romantic Pieces by Frantisek Max Knize
for Ukulele
Notebook for Anna Magdalena Bach and
Ukulele
Open Tunings for Ukulel (MB)
Robert Burns songs for ukulele
Jewish songs for C tuning ukulele
Campanella style songbook for beginner:
C tuning ukulele
Antonín Dvořák: opera The Jacobin for
ukulele
Leopold Mozart's Notebook for Wolfgang
Arranged for Ukulele (MB)
The canons for one or two ukuleles
Solo and Variations for ukulele volume 1.,
2., 3.
Czech Medieval Ukulele
Christmas Carols for ukulele
Harmonics for ukulele
43 Ghiribizzi by Niccolo Paganini for
Ukulele
Christmas Carols for Clawhammer ukulele
Gospel Clawhammer ukulele Solos
Czech Renaissance folk songs for Ukulele
Classical music for Clawhammer Ukulele
Christmas Carols for Crosspicking Ukulele
Josef Pekárek Two Hanakian operas
for Ukulele
How to play on three ukulele
simultaneously
Clawhammer solo for Ukulele
Gospel Crosspicking Ukulele Solos
48 Fingerstyle Studies for Ukulele
Compositions for ukulele
18 Dance Tunes from Caslav Region for
Ukulele
Francisco Tárrega for Ukulele (MB)
10 songs from the years 1899-1920 for
Ukulele
Czech Hymnbook for Ukulele
Campanella style songbook
for intermediate

For C tuning with low G
Irish tunes for all ukulele
Gospel Ukulele low G Solos
Antonin Dvorak: Biblical Songs: for
Ukulele with low G
Gregorian chant for Ukulele with low G
The Czech Lute for Ukulele with low G

Romantic Pieces by Frantisek Max Knize
for Ukulele with low G
Notebook for Anna Magdalena Bach and
Ukulele with low G
Robert Burns songs for ukulele with low G
Jewish songs for ukulele with low G
Campanella style songbook for beginner:
ukulele with low G
Czech Medieval Ukulele with low G
Christmas Carols for ukulele with low G
Fingerpicking solo for Ukulele with low G
43 Ghiribizzi by Niccolo Paganini for
Ukulele with low G
Christmas Carols for Crosspicking Ukulele
with low G
Czech Renaissance folk songs for Ukulele
with low G
Gospel Crosspicking Ukulele with low G
Solos
Josef Pekárek Two Hanakian operas for
Ukulele with low G
18 Dance Tunes from Caslav Region for
Ukulele with low G
10 songs from the years 1899-1920 for
Ukulele with low G
Czech Hymnbook for Ukulele with low G
Boogie woogie patterns for ukulele with
low G
Compositions for ukulele with low G
Second Fingerpicking solo for Ukulele
with low G
Double Stop Gospel for Ukulele
with low G

For Baritone ukulele
Irish tunes for all ukulele
Gospel Baritone Ukulele Solos
Antonin Dvorak: Biblical Songs: for Bari-
tone Ukulele
Gregorian chant for Baritone Ukulele
The Czech Lute for Baritone Ukulele
Romantic Pieces by Frantisek Max Knize
for Baritone Ukulele
Notebook for Anna Magdalena Bach and
Baritone Ukulele
Robert Burns songs for Baritone ukulele
Jewish songs for baritone ukulele
Campanella style songbook for beginner:
Baritone ukulele
Czech Medieval Baritone Ukulele
Christmas Carols for Baritone ukulele
Fingerpicking solo for Baritone ukulele
43 Ghiribizzi by Niccolo Paganini for
Baritone ukulele
Christmas Carols for Crosspicking
Baritone ukulele
Czech Renaissance folk songs for
Baritone ukulele

Gospel Crosspicking Baritone Ukulele
Solos
Josef Pekárek Two Hanakian operas for
Baritone Ukulele
18 Dance Tunes from Caslav Region for
Baritone Ukulele
10 songs from the years 1899-1920 for
Baritone Ukulele
Czech Hymnbook for Baritone Ukulele
Boogie woogie patterns for
Baritone Ukulele
Compositions for Baritone Ukulele
Second Fingerpicking solo for
Baritone Ukulele
Double Stop Gospel for Baritone Ukulele

For Baritone ukulele with high D
Jewish songs for baritone ukulele
with high D
Campanella style songbook for beginner:
Baritone ukulele with high D
Solo and Variations for Baritone ukulele
with high D volume 1., 2., 3.

For 6 sting ukulele (Lili'u ukulele)
Gospel 6 string Ukulele Solos
Gregorian chant for 6 string Ukulele
Notebook for Anna Magdalena Bach and 6
string Ukulele
Robert Burns songs for 6 string ukulele

For Slide ukulele (lap steel ukulele)
Comprehensive Slide Ukulele: Guidance
for Slide Ukulele Playing
Gospel Slide Ukulele Solos
Irish tunes for slide ukulele
Robert Burns songs for Slide ukulele

For D tuning ukulele
Skola hry na ukulele (G+W s.r.o.)
Irish tunes for all ukulele (CSI)
Jewish songs for D tuning ukulele (CSI)
Campanella style songbook for beginner:
D tuning ukulele (CSI)

Guitalele (Guitarlele)
Fingerpicking Guitalele Solo volume I. -IV.
Gregorian chant for Guitalele
The Czech Lute for Guitalele
Irish tunes for Guitalele
The canons for Guitalele
Gospel Guitalele Solos
Fingerpicking Guitalele Solo volume V. - Classical music
Czech Medieval Guitalele
Czech Renaissance folk songs for Guitalele
Robert Burns songs for Guitalele
18 Dance Tunes from Caslav Region for Guitalele

Czech Hymnbook for Guitalele
18 popular Czech Minuet for Guitalele

G tuning (gDGBD) Banjo
Czech Medieval G tuning Banjo
Classical music for Clawhammer G tuning Banjo
Gregorian chant for G tuning Banjo

For EADA tuning ukulele
EADA ukulele tuning
Gospel EADA Ukulele Solos

Ukulele Duets
Notebook for Anna Magdalena Bach, C tuning ukulele and C tuning ukulele
Notebook for Anna Magdalena Bach, C tuning ukulelé and Ukulele with low G
Notebook for Anna Magdalena Bach, C tuning ukulele and Baritone ukulele
Notebook for Anna Magdalena Bach, Ukulele with low G and Ukulele with low G
Notebook for Anna Magdalena Bach, Ukulele with low G and

Baritone ukulele
Notebook for Anna Magdalena Bach, Baritone ukulele and Baritone ukulele
The canons for one or two ukuleles
Mauro Giuliani arranged for Ukulele Duet (MB)
Notebook for Anna Magdalena Bach for Ukulele and EADGBE Guitar
Notebook for Wolfgang for Ukulele and EADGBE Guitar

New Diatonic Accordion (Melodeon) books
For G/C diatonic accordion
Bass songbook for G/C melodeon
Cross row style songbook for beginner
G/C diatonic accordion
Gospel G/C diatonic accordion Solos
9 songs from the years 1899-1920 for G/C melodeon
Czech Hymnbook for G/C melodeon
Songbook for G/C diatonic accordion *Volume 1. -2.*
18 popular Czech Minuet for G/C diatonic accordion
Robert Burns songs for G/C diatonic accordion
Jewish songs for G/C diatonic accordion

For C/F diatonic accordion
Cross row style songbook for beginner
C/F diatonic accordion
Gospel C/F diatonic accordion Solos
9 songs from the years 1899-1920 for C/F melodeon

For D/G diatonic accordion
Cross row style songbook for beginner

Kalimba
Songbook for Kalimba B11 Melody
Second songbook for Kalimba B11 Melody
Songbooks for Kalimba Am+G

D/G diatonic accordion
Gospel D/G diatonic accordion Solos
9 songs from the years 1899-1920 for D/G melodeon
Robert Burns songs for D/G diatonic accordion

New Anglo Concertina books

For C/G 30-button Wheatstone Lachenal System
Gospel Anglo Concertina Solos
Notebook for Anna Magdalena Bach and Anglo Concertina
Robert Burns songs for Anglo Concertina
The Czech Lute for Anglo Concertina
Gregorian chant for Anglo Concertina
Josef Pekárek *Two Hanakian operas* for Anglo Concertina

For C/G 20-button
Gospel C/G Anglo Concertina Solos
Robert Burns songs for C/G Anglo Concertina
Gregorian chant for Anglo Concertina

Czech Hymnbook for Alto *Hugh Tracey* Kalimba
Robert Burns songs for Alto *Hugh Tracey* Kalimba
Songbooks for Kalimba E116
Songbooks for Alto *Hugh Tracey* Kalimba

New Flute Recorder books
18 Dance Tunes from Caslav Region for Recorder Quartet
Josef Pekárek Two Hanakian operas for Recorder Quartet

Czech Medieval Songs For Two Recorders
Robert Burns songs for Recorder Quartet

Publishing House
CSI = CreateSpace Independent Publishing Platform
MB = Mel Bay Publications
G+W = G+W s.r.o.

Made in United States
North Haven, CT
17 February 2024

48856353R10028